"It's WEDNESDAY," said Peggy. "We'll stay home to-day,
And swing, oh so high, and with dollies we'll play."
And they "worked up" together—the swing flew so high,
They saw the white cloudlets at rest in the sky.

On THURSDAY they romped in the meadow, and found
Some dear little piggies at play on the ground.
The wee piggies squealed when they squeezed them in fun,
Then Mamma Pig came and the twins had to run.

On FRIDAY they carried a very big kite,
Out into the road, where they sent it in flight.
The Wind snatched it up, and tore it in twain,
And out of the clouds, came a downpour of rain.

A sunshiny SATURDAY filled them with glee,
They see-sawed, and laughed, and sang merrily.
The see-saw was old, and what do you think?
It split—and the twins fell, quick as a wink!

A Celebration of Twins

WELLERAN POLTARNEES

LAUGHING ELEPHANT

MMVI

ISBN-10 1-59583-055-3
ISBN-13 978-1-59583-055-5

LAUGHING ELEPHANT BOOKS
3645 INTERLAKE AVENUE NORTH   SEATTLE, WA 98103

WWW.LAUGHINGELEPHANT.COM

Life is a blessing, and, thus,
twins are a double blessing.

Though twins are much more
trouble to their parents,

the joyous satisfactions
more than make up for it.

Twins are lovely to behold,
for multiplicity adds delight.

Twins are seldom lonely.

They always have someone
to play with,

and talk to,

and to share their
triumphs and sorrows.

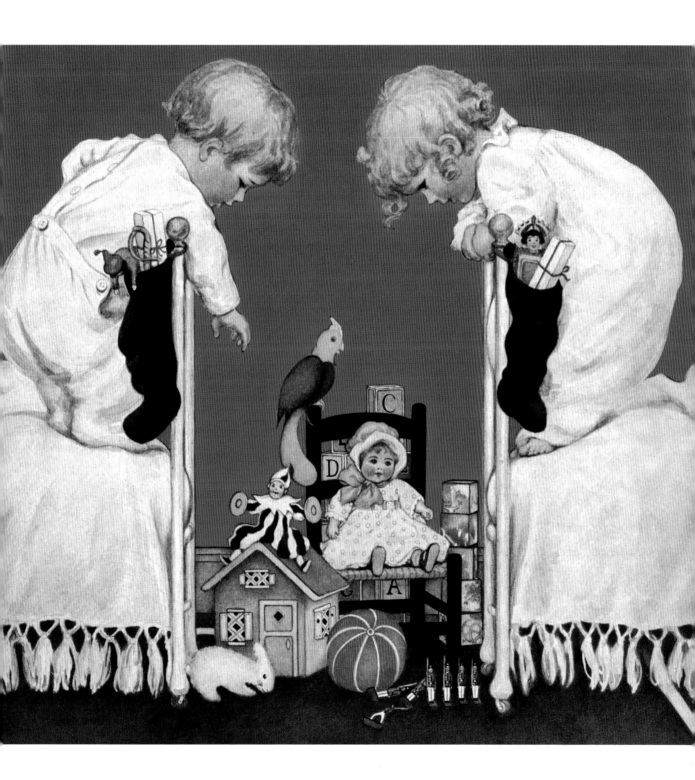

Twins teach each other,

confide in each other,

The Twins Vacation
by
Gertrude MacQuigg Warner
Each one of these Pictures was cut
out of black paper with a
scissors.

On SUNDAY the girlies were dressed in their best,
Their hearts full of joy, their minds quite at rest.
They hurried to Sunday School, both good as gold,
For the six coming days promised wonders untold.

On MONDAY the twins picnicked under the trees,
With a tiny tea table and seats, if you please.
And just as they came to the ice cream and pie,
A big, hungry, wicked old cow made them fly!

On TUESDAY they fished on the edge of the brook,
With a branch for a rod, and a pin for a hook.
But a spider scared Betsy.   She jumped with a scream,
And straightway they both tumbled into the stream.

and share the tasks of life.

Twins offer, each to each,
a secret understanding,

and face the world stronger
because of their twinship.

PICTURE CREDITS

Front Cover   Jessie Willcox Smith. Advertising illustration, 1925.

Endpapers   Unknown. From *John Martin's Big Book No. 5*, 1928.

Frontispiece   Inez Hogan. From *Bigger and Bigger,* 1942.

Title Page   Susan Beatrice Pearse. From *The Twins & Tabiffa,* c. 1935.

Copyright   Holling C. Holling. From *The Twins Who Flew Around the World,* 1931.

Page 1   Helen Sewell. From *The Princess and the Apple Tree,* 1925.

Page 3   Bertha Wegmann. "Maternity, n.d.

Page 5   Helen Sewell. From *The Princess and the Apple Tree,* 1925.

Page 7   Unknown. Advertising illustration, n.d.

Page 9   Ruth Cobb. From *Blackie's Children's Annual,* 1920.

Page 11   Inez Hogan. From *Bigger and Bigger,* 1 942.

Page 13   Corinne Pauli Waterall. From *The Twins Tom and Don,* 1940.

Page 15   Katherine R. Wireman. Magazine cover, 1915.

Page 17   Charlotte Becker. Illustration, n.d.

Page 19   Guy Pène du Bois. "Intellect & Intuition," 1918.

Page 21   Keith Ward. Advertising illustration, 1948.

Page 23   Unknown. From *Science All About Us,* 1946.

Page 25   Albert Herter. "The Bouvier Twins," c. 1926.

Page 27   Lewis Baumer. Advertising illustration, 1928.

Page 28   Max Hertwig. Advertising illustration, 1920.

Page 29   Micheline Boyadjian. "The Girls," n.d.

Back cover   Hazel Frazee. Magazine cover, 1934.

COLOPHON

This book is designed by Chev Darling & Moses Gershbein at Blue Lantern Studio.

Typeset in Poppl-Laudatio.